CHOOSING CRAZY OVER EASY

Choosing Crazy over Easy

Finding the Joy in Life's Hot Messes
(Even When You Have Other Plans)

WISE INK

CARLY-ANN DELL

ISBN-13: 978-1-63489-511-8

Library of Congress Catalog Number has been applied for.
Printed in the United States of America
First Printing: 2022

26 25 24 23 22   5 4 3 2 1

Cover and interior design by Patrick Maloney

Wise Ink Creative Publishing
807 Broadway St. NE
Suite 46
Minneapolis, MN 55413

For the "got it together" woman
who is a bit unstable at times
(and yeah, that's you too)

Acknowledgments

To the man who was my fiancé when I started out-lining this book. The man who became my husband when the chapters began to fall into place. The one who stood by my side as our world came crashing down and my words could no longer flow. The one who became a parent with me as the final words were put into place—the best father to our rainbow baby as the world reads this book.

Casey, mi amor, you are my rock. Thank you for pushing me. Thank you for making me a better person. Thank you for choosing crazy over easy with me.

And a huge thank you to everyone who helped make this book possible! From editing, to reading, to motivating me to keep going, I appreciate your help more than you know!

Disclaimer

This book is not intended for you and me to compare our rides on the Hot Mess Express. I *know* we all have round-trip tickets on that train. It is also not about lacking self-confidence, but rather acknowledging that we all feel a bit uncertain at times. Even though this book talks a lot about the anxieties and pressures of life, it is not meant to bring on anxiety! This book was written to let you know that from one somewhat-of-a-hot-mess to maybe another, you are not alone.

Prelude

The alarm goes off, you haven't even opened your eyes yet, and somehow you're already behind on your huge to-do list for the day.

For me, this seems to be a regular occurrence lately. The jitters pop up between taking the dogs out, making coffee, and prepping meals and bottles for the day, all while attempting to ignore the notifications on my phone as they alert me to the day ahead. When the anxiety starts to creep in, I remind myself about that morning routine I've been trying to nail down for the last three months—you know, the one where you start the day doing something for yourself before you actually start the day? I seem to be struggling in that department.

On this particular morning, I have a messy bun on top of my head, shirt down to my knees sufficing for pants as I take the dogs out. Formula powder has managed to end up all over the counter rather than in the baby's bottle, and I've burnt the toast to a crisp (some extra peanut butter will have to take care of that one today). For now, this is my current morning situation—tomorrow, I will do better! We are still going to "make it a great day," as my husband says, and set a positive mindset for the day—or at least that is what my self-help book of the month is telling me to do.

This might sound absurd to some of you, while others might be saying, "Yep, this is my morning!"

Despite how exhausting those words were to read (and to type!), I honestly don't see any of these so-called mishaps as negative anymore. Yes, they absolutely leave me a bit frazzled and disoriented, but this is part of my everyday life and journey. Sometimes we just have to "bless the hot mess"!

I have learned to embrace these hectic moments and take them for what they are. Sometimes I can laugh at them, sometimes I cry, and sometimes I have to remove myself from the situation entirely, but I have learned to love all the ups and downs of life, acknowledging that there are many moments of uncertainty. We are all just doing our best.

Don't worry, this book is not me unloading my dirty laundry or telling you how I'm more of a hot mess than you are. I'm here to help you learn to appreciate your own unique life (whether it's as chaotic as mine or not) and how to turn those unplanned mornings, moments of anxiety, and pressures of trying to tackle everything on your to-do list into learning experiences. I want you to honor your journey and embrace the struggle, because that is where growth begins. Most importantly, I want you to know you are not alone in these struggles and anxieties. I am here to tell you that regardless of our different journeys, we all can relate with one another in more ways than we may know.

I Dropped Out of Grad School

Yes, I did. It was the best decision for me, and I'm going to tell you why. Not only did I drop out of school, but I also left the country, started working for an international resort company, and fell in love with an older man. I know, someone call Nicholas Sparks!

I have always been type A—the rule follower, the first to raise her hand, the honor roll student. The one who does everything "right," never wants to get into trouble, and always wants to make others proud. It's exhausting! It was all I knew, so I just kept chugging along. Until I didn't.

We go through high school working to get into a good college; then we start college in an attempt to figure out what the hell we want to do with the rest of our lives. We declare the major, take the classes, and then convince ourselves that we have chosen the "right" career path, only to graduate and realize it's not enough. So then we apply for graduate school (because more schooling is always the answer); then, finally, we graduate with our master's, our path now clear. Right?

Oh wait, your story didn't go like that? The "right" path didn't present itself at the exact moment you needed answers and a direction? Good. Mine didn't either. That was the trajectory I thought I was *supposed* to follow, and to be honest, it was pretty accurate for a long time. I was the straight-A-student, looking-for-extra-credit, graduating-at-the-top-of-my-class type of girl. Then I dropped out of grad school. I was evolving, but I didn't see it that way at first.

Now, ladies (and gents), if you are still in school, or if your planned path looks something like the previous statement, this is *not* your okay to quit! I value education and would not be where I am today without it, but my train needed to take a detour, and I needed to allow this to be okay.

My struggle with perfectionism and living my life for others was taking over my every move, and I needed to jump on a different track.

However, if this resonates with you, I do challenge you to dig a little deeper and reevaluate the *why* behind the direction you are working so hard to reach. If you are loving your path but find it challenging, don't stop! Life is not intended to be easy! Find your why again. Use it to motivate you to keep pushing for your goals, understanding that while motivation will not always be there, the discipline you create along the way can help you reach the goal you are striving for.

If, on the other hand, you are completely unsure of your every current move and feel discouraged with where you see your life heading, don't worry—you are not alone. We'll chat about all this in its entirety when I talk about my quarter-life crisis—oh yes, my friend, that quarter-life crisis is *real*! But know that it's okay and, in my opinion, totally normal. We all have moments of doubt and uncertainty about the path our lives are headed down or the decisions we have to make in order to work toward our goals. As I stated earlier, the "right" path does not always present itself in a clear and concise manner. Sometimes, it is the detours that lead us along a road we never intended to take that ultimately help us find what we were looking for.

I never thought that my compulsion to be perfect and please others was an issue. I graduated with a degree in early childhood and family studies, then began pursuing my master's in school counseling. My passion and desire have always been to help people. I want to make a difference in the lives of others; at the time, I believed this was where I was meant to focus my energy and how I was going to fulfill my purpose. I completed the first year of a three-year program before I decided to drop out, leave the country, and start working for an international resort company called Club Med.

Let me emphasize, this was *not* easy for me! I am a homebody; I like when there are right and wrong (and clear!) answers. I thrive in school because there is a measurement of success through grades, and the unknown has always freaked me out a bit.

Sometimes, it is the detours that lead us along a road we never intended to take that ultimately help us find what we were looking for.

It's actually rather interesting that I'm writing a book—in school, I always excelled in math and science because the answers were clear. There was typically a right or wrong answer based on an equation, whereas in writing, I had to explain myself or dive deeper into a specific topic. At that point in my life, I needed and wanted clear and concise answers rather than reflecting on why I felt a certain way. That is probably why I stuck to such a rigid path for so long!

But here I was, twenty-three years old, about to hop on a plane to Cancun, Mexico, to take a position as a wakeboard and water ski instructor. Clearly my "purpose" to make a difference in this world was taking a bit of a turn. I had been ready to become a school counselor, hoping to help kids and young adults figure out what they wanted to do with their lives; now, here I was, unsure about my journey, instead buying a few swimsuits for my new daytime dress code. It's safe to say I was a little lost and confused, but sometimes getting completely lost is exactly what the soul needs in order to truly be found. (Spoiler alert: this is not the last time you'll read me being uncertain with my direction in life. Apparently, I really like to lose myself in order to find myself.)

What is it about life and society that makes us feel like we need to know exactly where we are and where we're going at all times? We have to have a job title and a purpose and constantly be "put together." If our direction in life is not clear to others, then we feel inadequate. We feel the need to be reassured and validated by others, and we assume holding a certain title will do that for us. The pressure can be overbearing at times and make us feel like we are not good enough. Who set these standards, though?

Ladies (and gents), *we* set these standards! *We* place these standards and expectations upon ourselves!

These usually unspoken standards are what we choose to believe others expect of us. Society might influence them, but we push ourselves *so* hard to be this perfect, put-together image when no one's expecting that from us! It's a never-ending tunnel, and the light at the end never seems to appear.

If dropping out of school taught me anything, it

was that our plan is not always clear. We are some-times in what feels like a waiting pattern until that next road divide comes along, but this does not mean we stop living. It also does not mean that we just stand and wait for something to happen! We live for that day and thrive in the unknown; we also say *screw it* to having it all figured out! If we are always so focused on "figuring it out," we live for tomorrow and don't truly enjoy today.

I always say, "Waiting is the hardest part." We do not want to be caught in seasons of life where we are simply waiting around for what might hap-pen next or what might present itself to us. In that case, we're missing out on portions of our life that we're meant to experience and grow from!

I believe it's important to recognize that the journey is in the struggle! Without the struggle, we would lack growth and understanding in so many facets of life. If the self-help book you are reading this month is telling you how to get from point A to point B, remember that once you arrive at point B, point C shows up! The next struggle and area of growth will present itself. We don't want to skip past these or wish them away. Appreciate the struggle!

I personally believe that God has a plan for all of us. He knows what our next move is long before it even becomes a dim shadow of an idea in our mind. If we are constantly trying to figure out our own plan, we might miss the plan He has already created for us.

I know this can be frustrating and truly defeating at times, knowing that what we want and are working so damn hard for might not manifest itself tomorrow. However, it's comforting to know that where we are at this specific moment is exactly where we are supposed to be.

> *"Life can only be understood*
> *backwards; but it must*
> *be lived forwards."*
> —**Soren Kierkegaard**

CHAPTER TWO

The Real versus the Ideal

Okay—before we really dive into this book, I feel as though I should share a little bit of my background. Don't worry, nothing too long-winded (I know you didn't purchase an autobiography), but here are the basics.

For starters, I am a bit of an idealist. Actually, let's be real, I am very much an idealist! I love to dream big and paint perfect scenarios in my head. I believe in fairy tales and romantic comedies; I'm from a small town where everyone knows everyone, your school counselor is also your basketball coach, and everyone marries their high-school or middle-school sweetheart. I don't know why, but the struggles and uncertainties of life didn't seem to present themselves when I was younger, or maybe I was simply never made aware of them. Looking back, I think everyone suppressed their

25

hard moments, allowing them to create the illusion that they had it all put together and were happy. That was easier than having a small town know about our individual issues.

Honestly, I loved growing up in a small town. I loved knowing my teachers in and out of school, I loved how the whole town came together for Friday night lights, I loved that you would run into your best friend's mom at the grocery store. But I think this also molded a lot of my idealistic thoughts and my need to follow a specific plan. That idealism often leads me to expect and/or hope that things will simply unfold a certain way or all fall into place, when that is not reality. While I might be an idealist and an optimist, I am also fully aware that nothing in life is perfect, and rarely do things happen exactly as we plan.

Since perfectionism is something that has consumed me for most of my life, I've often gone to the extreme of trying to make something fit the fairy-tale image of others' expectations I've fabricated inside my head. Whether it was staying in a relationship longer than I should have simply to have the high-school sweetheart story, going to grad school in order to earn a master's degree, or trying every diet in the book in hopes of being the smallest version of myself, I would continue to strive in the hopes of being perceived as "perfect." If I didn't believe I was the best at something, it often resulted in me changing direction or not even attempting to move forward in what I was trying to pursue. This compulsion consumed my dating life and my athletic abilities, and even impacted my major intended career path.

Seems pretty sad, huh? Honestly, looking back, it was. I don't even know if I had a sense of self during many of those seasons of life, because I was ultimately living for others and fulfilling their dreams, not mine. At the time, though, I genuinely did not see it. I enjoyed life so much—I felt happy, I loved school, I had great friends and family, and I never seemed to fully notice the pressures I was placing upon myself. I think I also assumed that since no one opened up about their personal struggles—or at least we didn't hear about them—it was possible that I was alone in the uncertainties and personal battles I was experiencing. So I simply continued moving forward, trying to be the person and student I assumed others expected me to be.

We all have different definitions of "perfect," but quite frankly, it just doesn't exist. Nor should it be something we are striving for! (But I'll touch on that more later.)

If you are anything like me, when you were younger, you had an age in your head by which you assumed you would have it all figured out, the pieces of your life all just falling into place. The job, the relationship, the kids, maybe some financial freedom, finally nailing down the diet of the month. Sound familiar?

As a woman in my thirties, I expected I would have it all figured out by now, but that is far from the truth!

When I met my husband, Casey, I saw a fairy-tale scenario unfolding. You see, my parents met working for Club Med, which was the same international resort company I was working for when I met Casey. They were about our age when they met, fell in love, and got engaged rather quickly.

They were actually living in different countries when they got engaged. My dad sent my mom a board game, and then every day for the next few weeks he sent game pieces to her, which resulted in him asking her to marry him. I know, pretty dang cute!

So there I was, falling for a man in another country in a very similar way to how my parents met and got engaged. But our story didn't unfold the same way—nor should it have, but sometimes when the bumps in the road of our relationship presented themselves, I would panic!

Casey is someone who takes one step when he is able to take five. And after years of being together, I love him for this! But as someone who wanted a perfect story to unfold, I found myself questioning everything.

"Are things going to work out?"

"Does he actually love me?"

"Do I want this more than him?"

"When will our relationship move forward?"

I think at times I was feeling a bit all over the place, purely driven by all my expectations and thoughts of the future!

We were living out of the country, for goodness' sake! We had *no* idea how we were going to function together in "real life" as opposed to on a beach at a beautiful resort. Most first dates don't take place on a beautiful beach inlet with a packed lunch and a bottle of spiced rum (even if they should!). And let's not forget, I had quite literally just run away from the life I had planned on pursuing back home.

Even then, wild as it is to admit this now, I had every intention of returning to my life back home, continuing with my master's, and moving forward with the life that I was mapping out for myself pre–Club Med. Little did I know a different, messier, and more exciting story was unfolding.

While my parents' story sounds like it was seamless and romantic, I know for a fact that it was not. But that is so much of life—it's a highlight reel.

It's important to remember that we only see the pieces of the puzzle people want to show us. We only hear the parts of the story that glorify the end result, and if we happen to hear about the bumps or the struggles, it is simply to help that final result shine a bit more! No one wants to air their dirty laundry (and truthfully, not many of us want to hear it), but I think we all find comfort in knowing that there is always more to the story than people choose to show. We all have fears and deal with the ups and downs of life, but it is those hard moments that shape us.

My life is a beautiful hot mess! It is almost the exact opposite of how I imagined it in my head, but doesn't that make it all the more exciting and fulfilling?!

Life is not one-size-fits-all. Thirty is not the magic age where we miraculously have it all figured out, and in today's fast-paced, social-media-soaked world, we get wrapped up in feelings of not being enough *or* feeling like we always need to be doing *more* because others are ten steps ahead of us. Everyone's journey is different, and comparing ourselves gets us nowhere.

Life is messy, unsure, and beyond chaotic at times! We need to learn to appreciate the unexpected, because when we embrace the moments that feel like a hot mess, we allow the person we are intended to be to finally start living.

To my younger self who assumed the small-town story was the only version that was meant to be written, I am so glad you kept dreaming life into a new chapter.

We need to learn
to appreciate the
unexpected, because
when we embrace
the moments that
feel like a hot mess,
we allow the person
we are intended to be
to finally start living.

CHAPTER THREE

You're a 9.9

I am perfect.

Or at least that's what I'm supposed to portray: good grades, put together, smile always on my face, following "the plan," boxes checked, and doing a pretty damn good job at keeping the assumptions of my perfection accurate.

In high school, this meant going above and beyond to get any extra credit necessary to ensure I would still have an A in the class after the final—not an A-, an A. In college, it meant choosing not to drink so that I could focus on my grades or be a better girlfriend in the long-distance relationship I was in at the time. In athletics, it meant playing every sport so that I could claim to be good at all of them but also have an excuse for why I wasn't the best at one in particular. On social media, it was fitting the aesthetic image I thought everyone needed in order to be "influential" or perceived as a "fitspo"—this despite how empty I felt inside not sharing the message to help others that was on my heart. When I think back on it, I probably left others thinking less of themselves because I held myself to such unsustainable standards.

Now, in my marriage, that perfectionism means waking up at 4:00 a.m. to start my morning, get the workout in, make the coffee, prepare my husband's meals for the day, and make sure to say that I slept great even though the to-do list played on repeat behind my eyes all night. And let's not even get me started on how this looks when it comes to my job—that would take an entirely separate chapter.

Now, you might be reading this and thinking, "Damn, she's type A," or, "Have your husband make his own damn lunches and coffee!" Or the need to do it all might resonate with you.

Maybe it's the extremes you go to for your boss. Maybe it's for your kiddos. Maybe it's in school and the career you're trying to map out for yourself. You feel as though nothing is ever "enough," and you are always striving to be "more." But "more" of what? "More" of who? We are all out here doing our best, yet we still continue to push ourselves beyond our limits.

Why? What is this driving force and need to be perfect?

Insecurities? Social media? Lack of confidence? Family? Friends? All of the above.

Don't get me wrong, I honestly enjoy most of these things! I enjoy being in the kitchen, waking up before the rest of the house, and making Casey's day easier by preparing a simple coffee and lunch before he heads off to work. I also find a lot of value in trying to show up as the best version of myself every day! But the problem is that I place pressure on myself, because now this is what's expected of me. Without it, I would be seen as less of a wife or "put-together" person.

Feeling like we have to do it all truly only leads to our own self-destruction. At some point, our cup will be empty, and we will have nothing to pour out. This realization often comes too late, or once a full-fledged breakdown is on the horizon. You know that breakdown I'm talking about. We feel it coming for days and know that a good cry would do us well, but for some reason we like to keep pushing our limits until we truly let the hot mess shine!

Our ability to do as many things as possible should not be a goal any of us strive for, yet somehow, we all find ourselves trying to do everything at once. So often, we try to multitask because we think this makes us a better person and adds more value to who we are. The truth of it is, we cannot do everything and do it all well.

I once read that many of us try to work on our weaknesses when we should be focusing on our strengths. If we put more time and effort into developing and growing our strengths, it would leave us with remarkable tools for life, rather than wasting time trying to sharpen a tool that is possibly not meant to be in our toolbox. Yet many of us continue to work ourselves into the ground trying to do it all and be the best in the process. We need to focus more on the things we are good at, the priorities that matter to us, and do them well!

Sometimes being "busy" does not mean we are

being productive. I have definitely learned this the hard way in the new "mom" season of my life. It is so easy to compare ourselves to others and what they might be doing in their everyday lives, but just because someone else is doing something does not mean we need to do it too. We simply are not meant to do it all!

It is imperative that we pour from a cup that has something in it if we want to adequately show up for others. If we are constantly pouring from an empty cup, this could lead to burnout, and it sure as heck does not allow us to show up as our best selves. I know it's easier said than done. It's easy to assume we can fill up our cup every day before something is needed from us, but my morning routine is most definitely not there yet!

So maybe this starts with us not simply pouring out our entire cup, instead allowing it to gradually become empty day after day. I personally believe this is a lifelong task and will look different in each season of life. Sometimes it might seem nearly impossible if not comical to actually have the time to fill up our cup, but the importance of it far outweighs the struggle.

Perfectionism is real. Not feeling like we are enough is real. Worrying about what other people think about us is real.

Something I have never fully admitted to anyone is that I changed my major my sophomore year of college because I was not getting the grades that fit my straight-A persona. The story I've told everyone is that I started to fall in love with my psychology classes and loved working with kids, so early childhood and family studies grabbed my attention. While this is true, it is not the entire story!

I went to the University of Washington with the intention of going into biology and later applying for the nutrition program or physical therapy program, but in the spring quarter of my freshman year of college, I had to take the class Biological Psychology. Just the name makes my head spin. Anyway, by the end of the quarter I was beyond drained and was finishing the class with a GPA that I was not proud of. It got me thinking about where I would graduate among my classmates and truly started to impact my potential career choices, all because of a numerical value.

Anyway, this led me to switch majors to something I knew would allow me to excel, as well as have a GPA that I could be proud of. Oh, and let's not forget, it allowed me to walk across the stage on graduation day with the cords stating that I had graduated cum laude.

Don't get me wrong, I truly love the direction I ended up going! I wouldn't be where I am today had I not changed majors. But it is sad and hard to admit that my need to be viewed as perfect was what caused me to change directions.

This had really started to consume me in my teenage years, when sports became a huge part of my life. I was fortunate to have athletics come rather easily to me, so I took part in many different activities. My issue was, once I excelled at a specific sport, I feared taking the next serious step forward. What if I couldn't live up to the expectations of being the best? What if I let down the people who expected so much of me?

This quite literally created paralysis in my athletic abilities. I would reach a certain point in my natural ability, then fear what it would look like if I didn't end up being the best. Rather than even try to be the best, I would slowly back away from the sport.

If I'm completely honest, we should always strive to be the best! Why would I want to settle for anything less than what I knew I was capable of? But fear took over.

I have always looked up to my dad. He goes to actual extremes (sometimes life-threatening!) to make sure he is showing up to the best of his ability. But when it comes to his business endeavors and athletics, he is next level. At a young age, it was his athletic ability that drove me and pushed me in sports, but that was also the leading cause of my sometimes holding back. He has been a competitive water skier for most of my life, and he is who I strive to emulate with my efforts in my sports and fitness journey.

If we are striving to be the best at something, it takes an entirely different level of commitment, and in hindsight, I never had that commitment. I would never admit that to anyone before now, but that level of commitment intimidated me.

What if I put in all the effort and still never became the best? What if I did all the work and still never made the team?

Lack of belief in myself and fear of failure consumed me. This would later transcend from sports to my fitness journey to my uncertainty within my own career goals.

But it really became prominent when I was fifteen years old, in a way that put a huge halt in my athletic career path. At the time, I was a competitive downhill snow ski racer. I loved it! It was a different sport than any of my other school friends took part in, so I couldn't compare myself to them, and I was good! Really good!

My sophomore year of high school, I qualified for the Junior Olympics. My training and natural ability were taking me in a direction I'd never imagined for myself. I was proud, excited, nervous, anxious—you name it—but this would also be one of the most pivotal times in my life thus far.

Soon after my qualification, my mind started to

take over. I placed limiting beliefs upon myself and assumed others were expecting me to all of a sudden be the best, rather than my best. I started to fall apart.

I went to the Junior Olympics and couldn't move. The first race of the weekend, I froze in the start gate and cried. I was consumed with fear and lack of confidence. I eventually pushed myself out of the gate, only to slide around a few turns and end up DFL—dead fucking last. (Excuse my language, but it's an intense sport, and this is actually a term we would use.) While it was a challenging course and the competitors were amazing, the truth was I had given up on myself before the race had even started. I assumed I wouldn't be the best, I assumed I wouldn't get first, so I convinced myself I wouldn't do well.

I'm not going to lie—I wouldn't have taken first, and I wasn't the best, but I was damn good! I deserved to be there! I'd earned the right to be there! Race after race, weekend after weekend of that entire season, I was working to be there! But my fear of not living up to the expectations of others, even at such a young age, was my downfall.

While the struggles of perfectionism are real, what is also real is our self-worth, our ability to be better for ourselves! We need to foster a habit of reframing the narrative—stopping the negative self-talk before it begins and replacing it with positive affirmations.

Growing up, my mom always told me that I was a 9.9. She said perfection did not exist, but as her little girl, of course I was as close as someone could get. She wanted to instill in me that no one is a 10, no one is perfect, and no one was asking or expecting that of me. My mom wanted me to know that perfection was not something that I should strive for in life; rather, I should show up as my best self. Looking back on it, I think the version of me others saw was genuinely my best self; I simply placed limiting beliefs upon myself and didn't see what others saw.

Potential is something we all have, but it is what we do with our potential that can make us great. How do we recognize that potential, then continue

While the struggles of perfectionism are real, what is also real is our self-worth, our ability to be better for ourselves!

to grow upon it throughout life and not get complacent? We all have that choice, but it is whether or not we choose to act upon it that separates many individuals.

One of my favorite business mentors, Emily Frisella, has a quote I love: "Don't have the potential of a freight train but live with the parking brake on."

We are that damn parking brake! Our own assumption or belief that we have to be perfect, the idea that everyone else is placing expectations on us—these are the little thoughts (brakes) that are holding us back from being who we want to be or living the life we know will leave us feeling more fulfilled and accomplished!

Let's remove that parking brake. Remove the need to please others. Get out of our own way and race down that hill.

So, make the cup of coffee for your husband, but make yourself one too, and enjoy every sip of it! You might still be in your pajamas, but you are showing up for yourself. One day at a time. One burnt piece of toast at a time. Embrace your unique journey.

I have been fortunate to be surrounded by hard-working individuals for most of my life. My parents have always worked their asses off, my coaches pushed themselves just as hard as they pushed me, and my mentors continue to educate themselves.

That said, it took me until now to realize they never asked for perfection. They asked me to show up. They asked me to be my best. They pushed me because they believed in me and knew what I was capable of.

> *"As we try to achieve perfection, society changes and we just become more imperfect."*
> **—Joao Matod**

As we continue to grow and allow our lives to evolve, expectations will change, goals will change, and the belief we have in ourselves will hopefully evolve for the better too. If we keep trying to strive for what others may perceive as perfect, we will miss an opportunity to grow and simply fall short on the next expectation of perfectionism.

Show up for the person you are hoping to become and take one small step every day to get closer to achieving it.

Show up for the person you are hoping to become and take one small step every day to get closer to achieving it.

CHAPTER FOUR

Diet of the Month

For as long as I can remember, most of my big life events were associated with a diet. Whether it was a dress fitting for a high school dance or the perfect spring break bikini, my mind was always occupied with a specific diet. I did it all—you name a diet, and I have tried it!

I remember dieting for the first time in middle school. I'd lie in bed at night praying to God to help me lose weight. I was always the short friend, but I seemed to hold onto that "baby fat" a lot longer than others. I grew up on a lake; the one-pieces slowly transitioned into bikinis, and it was cool for boys and girls to invite each other over to the water for their birthday parties. I was so embarrassed to be in my bikini, so I started to wear tankinis. Not even sure those are still around, but I loved them! I swear I had them in every color and pattern, and

I think they even had boob cups in them. I was in middle school and already so hyper-aware of my size and image.

After that first summer of really noticing my physical appearance, I wanted to know how I could lose weight. This is when I first learned about the whole 1,200 rule. Are you familiar with this number? Where did it come from? Why is 1,200 calories this magic diet number?

Anyway, soon all food became a number to me. I would simply turn over the package and read the big numbers to see how many calories were in each item. All my meals became math problems, and I almost saw it as a challenge to see if I could eat under 1,200 calories a day.

This started the yo-yo dieting for me. I soon learned that I could not function on 1,200 calories, but I would stick with it during times when I was desperate to lose weight. I pulled this handy tool out before all high school dances, on spring break trips, and every summer because we lived on a lake. I used this technique all the way through college and into my adult life.

My "fitness journey" and Instagram journey actually all started from a workout challenge. In order to be a part of the challenge, you needed to share your progress on social media. Prior to the start, we had to fill out a goal sheet which we could look back on throughout the challenge to keep us motivated. When asked to write my goal, I said it was "to be able to run in a sports bra and to have my boyfriend find me attractive." My desire to be able to run in a sports bra implied that my stomach would not jiggle when I ran. This was well before high-waisted workout pants were in, so the belly was just always out. I envied every woman with a flat stomach and desired it with all of my being.

The part about me wanting my boyfriend to find me attractive is what truly breaks me. It reflects the extreme lack of confidence I had in myself as a person. I looked over every other aspect of myself and held all my value in my size. That boyfriend is now my husband, and to this day I don't think he knows I wrote that down as my goal, but I also know that he would find me just as beautiful regardless of my weight because he sees me for me, not for my size.

This is important to remember: Those that love us and those that know us do not see our size! They do not see what we assume to be flaws; they simply see us and the value we add to their life. I know for a fact that the person I am when I am dieting or trying to be the smallest version of myself is not my best self, and it sure as hell is not the version that my husband fell in love with.

When it comes to dieting, ultimately the best diet is the one you can adhere to—and let me tell you, I could not adhere to any of my eight- to twelve-week diets. Once one was over, I had zero self-control and simply yo-yoed until the next started.

However, when I am eating well and working out, I am hands down a better version of myself! I am clear headed, energized, and pushing hard to show up for myself day in and day out! This has become a lifestyle; it has become about mindfulness and sustainability rather than attempting to end the day consuming as few calories as possible.

For me, the word "diet" means temporary. It is not something I plan on turning into a lifestyle. I

Those that love
us and those that
know us do not
see our size!

really value my health and fitness, but for the first time, I now see health and fitness as two different things. Health encompasses everything: mental, physical, emotional, and spiritual work, not just a number on a scale. Fitness pertains to the movement I choose to do every day, not a penalty. My workouts are no longer a form of punishment, and food is no longer a fear.

Health and fitness did not separate themselves in my life until recently. It slowly started before I got married, when I noticed a huge decline in my mental and emotional well-being. I had been so hyper-focused on my image and size for so long that I overlooked the other aspects of my health outside my physical state.

This understanding of health as a multitude of factors became even more prominent after having our son. This little human needed me in a way I had never been needed before; it was so joyful, yet also overwhelming and exhausting. I noticed that taking care of my mental and emotional health was starting to get put on the back burner again, and I quickly recognized the effort I needed to put in to make sure that did not happen.

I was finally in a season of life where health needed to encompass all aspects—physical, mental, emotional, and spiritual—in order for me to show up as my best self that day for this little human.

Not all of us will need to go through emotional breakdowns or have a kiddo to realize there needs to be a shift in our health and fitness journey. But if your diet or the lifestyle you are trying to create is consuming your every thought, your every move, and keeping you up at night with anxiety, you might need to reevaluate. Don't get me wrong, I think it is crucial to consider our overall health—I think we live in a society where many of us should take our training and nutrition into more consideration, but I also think we live in a society where we do not add mental and emotional well-being into the term "health."

It is undeniable that I am a better version of myself when I make movement and nutrition a priority. It is undeniable that I wake up with more energy and zest for life rather than feeling sluggish and drained. Feeling strong, empowered, and energized does not come from my desire to be the smallest version of myself; it truly is fueled by wanting to be the best version of myself!

Finding a balance within training and nutrition is not easy. Finding excuses tends to be the easier task. It's easy to toss around the word "lifestyle" and assume that means we'll stick to the plan during the week but then push it aside on the weekends. This is how many of us define "lifestyle," me included! Heck, I'll take an extra round of margaritas with chips and salsa any day!

But at some point, we have to sit back and be honest with ourselves. We have to ask ourselves the hard questions. Are we showing up for ourselves? Are we putting in the work that allows us to create the lifestyle we are striving for? The excuses get easier to create, and the happiness and balance we are seeking slowly slip away.

Training and nutrition look different for everyone throughout their lives; you're not going to have the same regimented routines forever. I learned that very quickly after I had our son, Cayden. I assumed I could go back to my old routine once I got the hang of mama life. I figured meal prep would fall back into play, that waking up early would get easier, but that has not been the case. It has all been hard! But most things that we care about take effort and do not come easily.

I have had to take moments of self-reflection to actually be honest and decide if I am putting in the work to my full potential or letting excuses slide in.

Stop making excuses! The home gym will never be quite big enough. The kiddo will never take the long nap you planned for. Your dog will not quietly lie on the floor next to you, but rather will be on your back during planks. You will be tired! Whether it is before work or after work, you will be tired! So, choose your tired!

If you are a new mama, sleep! Your excuse is actually a valid reason. If you are injured, your rest and recovery is a priority. But at what point do we recognize that other "reasons" are actually excuses?

You might be asking yourself why I added an entire chapter about dieting into this book. The answer is that when I think of "hot mess," the first thing I think of is my dieting past.

Many of you reading this might recognize that your dieting history has defined prominent moments of your life as well. Maybe you have missed out on moments that could have become memories, maybe you have devalued who you are as an individual based on your size or the number the scale reflects, or maybe you actually started living because you took your health into your own hands!

How we show up for ourselves is going to look different for everyone and will also change with each season of life. But if we all take a step back, we can agree that our overall health, both mentally and physically, is often what dictates how we show up as our best self.

So ask yourself, when is your dieting going to stop? When is your lifestyle going to start? What tired are you going to choose? Which hard are you going to choose?

Like most things in life, it won't be easy! But I am sure the person you start to show up as once you take control of this part of your life will be worth it!

> *"Marriage is hard. Divorce is hard. Choose your hard. Obesity is hard. Being fit is hard. Choose your hard. Being in debt is hard. Being financially disciplined is hard. Choose your hard. Communication is hard. Not communicating is hard. Choose your hard. Life will never be easy. It will always be hard. But we can choose our hard. Pick wisely."*
> —**Unknown**

Let's intentionally choose our hard and really start living.

CHAPTER FIVE

Seeking Balance

What is it about the word "balance" that almost instantly sends me into a state of anxiety? I feel as though it is something I should be striving for daily—once I achieve it, I will have life figured out. This is when everything will finally fall into place and a sense of peace will be instilled within me . . . right?

Wrong. Say it with me: there is no such thing as balance!

I always assumed that by age thirty I would have a pretty good grasp on life and my longing for balance would finally have been fulfilled. Thirty years old is clearly the magical number of life, so of course whatever "balance" is would be figured out by then. I never considered all the areas of life I would be trying to seek balance in over time—but what does "balance" even mean? I think for most of us, it is a struggle to define, and most definitely looks different from one person to the next.

One definition of balance is "an even distribution of weight enabling someone or something to remain upright and steady." Sure, that's what Merriam-Webster says, but when it comes to humans and just living life, balance isn't something you can achieve.

Please tell me it's not just me who feels as though I am never upright and steady. Something is constantly pulling me one way or the other!

For most of my life, I looked at balance as a ripple effect. Once I achieved balance in one area of my life, I could then start working on seeking it in another area, and so on and so forth, until it was established throughout my everyday life.

I'm almost laughing as I type this because I was so wrong! But that's me looking backward, and we all know that hindsight is 20/20. So how did I assume this ripple effect would start? I thought it all started with my physical appearance; the extent to which this consumed me was clearly outlined in the previous chapter.

Since body image and my size were weights for most of my life, I placed a strong focus on my fitness for a period of time. I leave out the word "health," which seems to get tagged alongside "fitness" as if they are a pair; in my case, "health" correlated with my size. The smaller I was, the healthier I was, and the more physically fit I must have been.

While I was attempting to reach this smallest version of myself—this took place many times throughout my life, might I add—I assumed that I could pour all my focus into workouts and minimal eating, pushing aside social engagements and family outings. I would go so far as to structure my time accordingly to ensure that my workouts and meals were planned out prior to agreeing to any social events. Once I achieved the body and image I was striving for, I would finally feel balance within my fitness journey, allowing me to have a social life again.

Truthfully, I thought I was thriving! Eventually I had the body I had been working on for so long and was now able to enjoy some friends and family time (with a Tupperware meal, of course).

I am someone who thrives on goals! So in that moment, this didn't seem to be a problem. I wanted to be where I was in my fitness, I wanted to push myself in my workouts like I never had before, I wanted to be intentional about my training and nutrition goals. At the time, however, I did not realize what I was sacrificing, or how my assumption that I would be able to balance it all moving forward would simply send me into a spiral that I was not prepared for.

Don't get me wrong, there are absolutely times in our life where a specific goal might consume us! Relationships get pushed to the side, social events are far and few between, and our whole life revolves around one specific target. This might even be a health and fitness goal that you have been wanting to accomplish! Having goals is so valuable to me and is truly what helps push me through life and holds me to a higher standard. Something about working toward a goal that seems so unattainable and then accomplishing it is beyond rewarding! But typically, when we are striving for these specific goals, balance is not something we are trying to obtain.

I eventually reached a place and time in life where I was craving balance. I wanted the body and the date night without the side of guilt, but I could not seem to figure out what that looked like or how and when I would be able to achieve it.

I remember the very first time Casey called me on a Friday evening and asked if I would meet him at our local Mexican restaurant for some tacos and a drink. I was excited because we did not do this often. After the evening was over, he told me it was the first time he had ever spontaneously asked me to meet him for a meal because I was always dieting or tracking my food. He told me he loved how I was goal oriented and always respected my drive and passion to push myself, but it definitely made me reflect on moments and memories I knew I had missed out on.

If you are anything like me, you like things to unfold according to your plan. Like I said, I'm type A, so I like to have control in all areas of my life. As you also might remember, I am an idealist, so I often find myself believing things will go according to the expected plan.

I truly thought that achieving a sense of "balance" in all areas of life would bring a sense of calm to my everyday life. If I am balanced, then I am in control, and if I am in control, then I feel balanced. The cycle continues.

So, what happens when something new is added to our lives? What happens when things change?

Maybe it's having a kiddo. Maybe it's getting a sweet pup. Maybe it's being in a serious relationship for the first time. Maybe it's landing that promotion you have been waiting for. What does this balance look and feel like in your life?

When I finally took a step back from my plans of achieving "balance," I realized that it was going to be ever changing.

Balance is not a destination, nor is it something that we achieve once, remaining "upright and steady" afterward as we move forward throughout life. It's okay to be on a teeter-totter, because life's all about the ups and downs and how we handle them.

Balance is not a destination, nor is it something that we achieve once, remaining "upright and steady" afterward as we move forward throughout life. It's okay to be on a teeter-totter, because life's all about the ups and downs and how we handle them.

Little adjustments have to be made each and every day in order for us to get daily tasks accomplished or handle the unplanned moments that pop up throughout the day. Things also look completely different from one life to the next!

With social media, we see the parts of other people's lives they choose to show us; we unknowingly take in a stranger's day-to-day life and wonder how they are able to do it all. We see them juggling work while still having time to pull themselves together. We see them have the kiddos, grow the business they started from scratch, get the morning workout in, and somehow manage to get a homemade meal on the table.

Most of us turn inward and compare others' highlights with our inability to show up for our life or our day with such ease, but we forget that we do not know the whole story. We also do not know how long it took for them to figure out their unique routine and manage it all.

So many important events in my life have been missed because I felt as though I were not "put together" or "presentable" enough for my age or life stage. I always felt the pressure of "seeking balance" to feel at peace with the direction my life was going in. I even felt this with some of my best friends, and still do to this day! I do not have a specific job title to share with them, we do not own our home, and my house is somewhat of a mess at all times. Even with the people who I know love me beyond all that, I feel as though I am not presentable enough. This has actually held me back from joining in on some of our get-togethers over the years! But if I step aside from my own need to achieve balance, I am able to see that maybe they are trying just as hard to achieve balance in their own lives!

Let me tell you: I am in my thirties, I am married, we have two dogs and a baby, and I have no idea how the hell I got here! But I can guarantee you it did not include balance. Gosh, most days I feel as though I am moving backward and upside down with no sign of putting pants on, but somehow tomorrow shows up and we try to do it all over again, just a little bit better than the day before.

I know for a fact I did not get to this place in

my life by trying to finish each day "steady and upright." I got here by living each day and making a lot of mistakes!

Do not fear making mistakes! Do not fear the road less traveled. The unknown will always be present. Each season of life will bring on more unknowns, which is part of the amazing ride of life!

Allow balance to be something you create within your life.

> *"Balance is not something you find; it is something you create."*
> **—Jana Kingsford**

Don't compare your life to others', because your choices and passions and fears are unique—you have your own life to live. Don't spend your time seeking out balance in order to find peace.

As my good friend Stacey Ervin Jr. says, "Ride the wave." Ride the wave of life! Create your life. Create your balance. And take it all one day at a time.

CHAPTER SIX

Finding Yourself Once You Remove the Titles

You know that one thing that always seems to pop up when a conversation is slowing down or becoming awkward, or when someone thinks they are trying to get to know you better? It's that damn question: "So, what do you do?"

As a grad-school dropout traveling the world and falling in love, my response to this question for a while was fun and exciting! It always led to an even better conversation and a very interested listener. But that was not always the case, especially when I moved back home and "reality" sank in. Once "adulting" set in, this question soon became an easy way to press my buttons.

For me, this is where my quarter-life crisis hit hard. I had just started grad school; I was not entirely sure why I was there. I thought I would have my life freak-out around forty years old, not twenty-three years old! But there I was; my heart was not entirely in it. I felt like I was there because it was the next thing I was supposed to do according to this plan I had created for myself in my head.

I had always assumed that after college my career path would be clear, and I would be in a relationship that would one day end in marriage. I thought life would just simply unfold. But as you know, that was not my story, and I don't think it is the story for many of us!

Those first couple years out of college are so hard! We're still figuring out who we are as young adults, we're just beginning to truly navigate life on our own without the structure of school, and there are so many unknowns ahead!

Maybe you're still in college and feeling this right now, or maybe you can also reflect on this season of your life and vividly remember the level of uncertainty you had taking that next step in an unclear direction. We search for titles such as "college graduate," "homeowner," "girlfriend," "Mrs.," "mom," "dad," "doctor," "manager," "CEO," etc. in order to define ourselves. When they are not there, it leaves us with a sense of emptiness.

Whenever someone asks the question, "So what do you do?" I find myself getting annoyed and in my head thinking, So what do I do, you ask? Well, for fun? For workouts? For sleep? For entertainment? Oh right, you mean for work!

This question should not be such a big trigger for me, but I'm never entirely sure how to answer it. I don't know if my response is interesting enough or good enough to obtain the interest of the listener. My path in life was always so clear; then I chose the road less traveled, which I am so thankful for, but I ended up with a life that I am still learning to navigate. I'm still not entirely sure what I am doing some days!

I am not ashamed of my path or my career! I am so happy with how things unfolded for me and so proud that I let them take a direction I was not prepared for. Still, this question creates struggles for me. Nevertheless, I take a deep breath and put a smile on my face before responding proudly.

My response does not consist of a clear, concise title that might help others understand what exactly I do for a living, but I make an effort to explain that I am working hard, providing value to my life as well as the lives of others, and being productive each and every day in my line of work.

Over time, I have concluded that this question gets to me because my response is not clear and concise. For the majority of our lives, we have simple yet meaningful responses to this question. In high school, we are students trying to figure out an interest that we might choose to dive into more in college. Maybe we play a sport or two or are in a club, which makes our response a little more exciting. In college, we are working toward declaring a major and possibly have a job that we can mention. After college, we hope to have a career that defines us or at least gives an intriguing response to this question of "what we do." Later on in our lives, we are supposed to be able to talk about our family or children, which seems to always keep a conversation going. But I struggled with feeling like my answer to this question was not worthy enough to share without adding extra "fluff" to my response.

Clearly this question rubs me the wrong way and probably bothers me more than it should, but for some reason I have always disliked titles and their implied definitions. This most likely stems from my assumptions that others are always placing expectations on me, so if my answer is not up to their standards, then it leads to insecurities within myself.

No matter where I've lived or what I've been doing, I have always searched for a title to define me. Despite disliking titles, I have felt as though I needed one to help answer this dreaded question and allow me to feel like I have a "place" in society.

Many of us often feel like we need to have a title or a specific niche that defines us. Whether it is within our line of work, our community, or just our families, a title gives us a sense of belonging. But what about those transitional periods of life? There are a number of times throughout our life when we are unsure of where we fit in, when we feel like we're just floating out to sea. We all desire to feel that sense of belonging and be accepted, so we try our hardest to find our "thing."

As I get older and repeatedly try to define my place in the world, I strongly believe that our purpose is often much bigger than we are able to see at any exact moment during our journeys. I'm beginning to realize that for many of us, our purpose and impact is outside our education and/or line of work. This is hard to comprehend at a young age, though. Many of us just spent the majority of our lives in school, hoping to have a solid answer to this question, only to find out that our purpose, passion, and work may all be unrelated.

But why do we feel the need to have a response that is going to impress others? We so badly want to sound intelligent or successful or interesting on some superior level. We desperately want to belong! But for what? For whom?

Like I stated earlier in this book, I loved school because there was a measuring scale. There was something to define your success. Whether it was through grades or your rank in your class, you had something to show for the work you were doing day in and day out. In everyday life, however, the ranking system or success scale is measured not in grades, but something else entirely.

Questions of measurement or rank that come to my mind are, "How much money do you make? How many followers do you have? Are you married? Do you have kids? Do you want kids? Do you plan to finish your master's program?" The answers are so different from one person to the next, but for each of us, one or more of these questions places an expectation or assumption on us that we sometimes feel we cannot live up to.

Maybe we can't have kiddos. Maybe we are struggling to have them but choose not to share about it. Maybe we don't want them. Marriage might not be a personal desire, or our career might no longer make us happy.

A lot of these scenarios and questions can lead us to believe we are not enough, or we are not on the intended path others expect of us.

Once I moved back from Club Med and found myself in "reality" without specific structure present, the assumption that I needed to have things figured out or bear specific titles created a lot of anxiety for me.

For the majority of our lives, structure is instilled in our routine without us even knowing it. At a young age, our daily schedule is created by our parents; soon after that, we head off to school. Most of us then spend thirteen years in school from kindergarten to twelfth grade, where nearly our entire day is planned out for us. If you decide to go to college, there are another four years or so with a schedule ingrained into your daily living, and possibly even grad school after that.

Without our even trying, a huge portion of our life is being dictated for us. We have to plan the rest of our life around school, but that's a constant that we can plan on and expect. Then what? We have just spent nearly our entire life having something else create routine and structure in our lives, and now it is gone.

The anxiety I placed upon myself was simply my assumption that I needed to have a title. I needed to have it all figured out in order to have a suitable response to the damn question of what I was doing with my life. But a quote I have held close for the last few years is, "Being a leader doesn't require a title; having a title doesn't make you one."

Just because we don't have a title that is clear or fully developed yet doesn't mean we don't have things figured out. It doesn't mean we are not waking up intending to be the best we can be.

Not knowing where we fit in or having a specific title does not take away from who we are as a person or where our journey in life is headed, just like having a title does not mean we have life figured out.

Allow your purpose to be bigger than a title. Allow your daily efforts to push you toward your goals and let your dreams be bigger than the expectations of others. You define your life. You define your success. You create your titles.

What if removing the titles finally allowed us to find ourselves? What if we were able to know who we are without a title defining it for us? Or what if we finally realized that maybe we have a number of titles!

Becoming a mom has illuminated how many

Allow your
purpose to
be bigger
than a title.

different hats I wear throughout the day and how much better it feels to not have a single specific "title" that defines me. I do not need to remove one hat to wear another, and carrying one hat does not make me any less capable of carrying another.

I proudly hold the title of "hot mess," and I am okay with that! I show up every single day a little unsure of my direction in life, and I am okay with that! I get to grow my dreams every day! If I held on to the expectations of others, I would have finished my master's program, become a school counselor, and never taken the time to lose myself a bit in order to find myself.

Instead, I am in my thirties, a new mom, happily married, navigating my way through my goals of entrepreneurship and dreams that currently seem out of reach. It is okay to have some of it figured out, yet still be a bit unsure of where things are going.

I no longer want my response to the question of "So, what do you do?" to fit into a specific box. I want to be all over the damn page with exciting responses that scare me a little bit. These moments that we often perceive as a challenge are actually pivotal points in our lives that we get to learn and grow from.

Appreciate the hot mess! Appreciate the struggle. Don't allow yourself to fall victim to searching for that perfect title, because the only title that you need is your name. You do you! You be you!

These moments that we often perceive as a challenge are actually pivotal points in our lives that we get to learn and grow from.

CHAPTER SEVEN

According to My Therapist

Did you know that it is okay to ask for help? Did you know that it is okay to need help—that life is not meant to be tackled all on our own? I didn't. Instead, I spent the majority of my youth and early adult life trying to be the anomaly of a person who did everything on her own.

Before jumping into my time with a therapist, let's all take a moment to thank someone we know we should be paying double: our hairdresser!

Whether or not you have been to therapy or are currently seeing a therapist, I think we can all admit that we should be paying our hairdresser double for his or her services! This is where the hot mess shines!

Who else spills the tea to their hairdresser? You walk in the door, sit down in the chair, and it's as if life becomes clear—you're finally ready to discuss all your troubles and sorrows. Just me? I didn't think so. I swear I should be paying my hairdresser for the services of being both my therapist and my hair stylist!

It is not until I sit down in the chair that I realize how much I have been holding in. Whether it is mentally, emotionally, or physically, it's as though things finally present themselves in a way that allows me to put words to what I am thinking and feeling.

I don't know if it's the number of hours I know I'll be sitting there that allows me to create conversation, filling the time by unloading all my dirty laundry, or if it's my genuine need to open up and talk to someone about everything on my heart and mind. Honestly, it's probably a mix of both. But within minutes, I always start to feel better because I am finally getting things off my chest that have been weighing on me for quite some time. Often they're small things, but those tend to be the thoughts and feelings that add up over time and then create stress and anxiety, which usually ends up leading to a breakdown.

I should be able to open up and spill all this to my therapist, but there's something about the comfort of my hairdresser that allows me to just speak my mind. But why do we feel the need to hide our dirty laundry until the last possible minute? Why do we feel the need to hide it at all? I see my hairdresser maybe twice a year, and holy heck, do I apparently keep a lot in until those visits with her!

We all struggle from time to time, we all have things we would like to do and be better at, and we all know that nothing and no one is perfect! So why do we try to be perceived as having it all put together?

Let me tell you, this girl does not have it all put together and will be the first to admit that! But I also know that I don't like admitting all my struggles until I'm sitting on that chair, staring back at myself in the mirror.

I am sure a lot of us don't want to put our "burdens" or "issues" onto others, so we bottle them up. We "deal" with them in a way we see fit. For most of us, that means suppressing these thoughts and emotions and pressing on as though we are perfectly fine. But why can't we normalize the hot mess a bit more? Why can't we normalize the fact that we all need to let out these thoughts and feelings from time to time?

There finally came a point where even adding an extra hair appointment wasn't going to help ease my anxieties and worries. I no longer saw my struggles as a burden but rather needed, and wanted, to work through the problems I was attempting to deal with on my own.

Let me paint you a little picture. It was the spring before my twenty-ninth birthday. I was in easily the best physical shape of my life. I was engaged to my best friend and the man of my dreams. All the planning was coming together beautifully for our destination wedding happening winter of the following year. The dress was picked out, the invitations were sent. My business was slowly picking up and becoming everything I had envisioned it would be within the first year that I truly let my passion take over. And then there was me—numb to it all. Nothing. No feelings or emotions toward anything.

Remember when I mentioned earlier in the book that my train would derail a couple times? This was another one of those times. I was nearing the end of my twenties and realizing that I wasn't capable of doing life all on my own. I could no longer carry the weight of trying to be perceived as perfect. The image and story from the outside perspective may have looked very put together, but on the inside, I was falling apart.

For most of my life, it has not been easy for me to ask for help. I never saw asking for help as a bad thing, but for some reason I assumed I needed to be able to do everything on my own (let's be honest, it was probably because I wanted to impress others). Now here I was, approaching my thirties, thinking I had it all figured out and everything was finally falling into place—and I was the most unhappy I had ever been.

I remember calling my parents and asking to meet with them because I knew I needed to get these feelings, or lack thereof, off my chest. I was ashamed to open up to my fiancé because I didn't want him to think less of me for needing to seek help. I had never been to therapy before and still had my own judgment around the concept of therapy. So, I reached out to the two individuals who knew me best.

One thing that's incredible about parents is that they usually want to help us feel better and figure out the solution to the problem at hand. But for the first time in my life, that itself was the issue. My parents were wonderful and listened to everything I had to say, but while I was sitting there, telling them that I felt numb and couldn't summon an emotion if I tried, they were trying to fill me up by reminding me of all my great qualities and everything wonderful I had going on in my life.

Sitting there, I was reminded of my relationship, my loving husband, my beautiful wedding around the corner, my exciting business ventures, and the hardest one for me to wrap my head around at the time: that my parents thought of me as a light that added so much to the lives of others.

This is where I felt the divide for the first time. There is a very strong difference between knowing and believing. I can know all these things. I can know I am a great person; I can know that I am working hard every day to move myself forward; but I do not always believe it.

Knowing and believing are two entirely different concepts, especially when it comes to self-confidence.

> *"Confidence is an inside job . . .*
> *Confidence is within you. Only you can*
> *cultivate it. You can't buy it and no*
> *one can give it to you, and the truest*
> *form is knowing who you are. What*
> *you stand for and what you allow."*
> **—Emily Frisella**

There I was, though, looking to my parents for some sort of validation. Prior to this, they were usually able to help me "snap out of it" and re-instill some belief within myself, but I was finally realizing that this was going to be an "inside job." I began searching for a therapist.

This was really hard for me. I am sure it has

Knowing and believing are two entirely different concepts, especially when it comes to self-confidence.

something to do with society and how it has impacted my view of therapy, but I assumed seeing a therapist meant something was wrong with me—that I was weak or unstable, possibly both! It feels strange to state now that my views on it have changed entirely, but for a very long time I was ashamed to admit I was going to therapy.

There was, and still is for many, a taboo around therapy. Similarly to how I felt, I think many of us assume going to therapy means there is something "wrong" with us. In reality, it is probably the best thing many of us can do in order to be our best self.

Seeking help is necessary for so many of us! Asking for help is crucial when life feels heavy like it's too much to handle! We are not meant to do life alone, and receiving help when we need it allows us to move forward and grow!

Having it all figured out is not the goal. Being put together and having the story unfold exactly as we intend is simply not reality. My idealist tendencies were causing me to feel trapped within my own story.

If confidence is within us, we need to know and

believe who we are! Not the person society wants us to be, not who our parents expect us to be, not who social media thinks we are. We need to cultivate it.

Don't be afraid to put in the work! Don't be afraid to take that first step and do something about it. No one has it all figured out, regardless of what "it" might look like. Life is about constantly evolving, facing challenges, and accepting change. This can be part of the beauty of life if we allow it to be. It's the continuation of growth and learning.

Pushing aside my stubborn tendencies and desire to do everything on my own was the moment I finally began to see who I was as an individual. Once I finally sought help from someone else, I truly began to become my own person.

Ask for help! Humans are designed to lean on one another. Let yourself seek out and accept that support; you won't regret it.

CHAPTER EIGHT

Support versus Validation

Therapy cleared up a lot for me. It helped bring many of my limiting beliefs to the surface and allowed me to recognize many areas in my life where I was seeking validation rather than support.

I was in a time of my life where many things were changing, and my ability to process that was lacking. Change is something I have always struggled with. Here I was about to make very permanent changes—ones that I was so excited about but struggling to process.

I think we easily find ourselves overwhelmed with emotions from time to time. Our inability to process those emotions or put words to how we are feeling can lead us to break down or shut ourselves off from others.

In these moments of uncertainty, self-doubt, or fear of change, we turn to those in our life that we love and trust to help instill confidence in ourselves and the decisions we are making. There have been many pivotal moments throughout my life where I chose to not make a decision until I had the support of everyone in my life.

I assumed a lot of this was from a lack of self-confidence or from insecurities I have carried for a majority of my life, but it came down to my misconception of support versus validation. Was I asking for loved ones' support in my decisions, or was I just needing their validation that my decisions and choices were up to their standards?

According to Oxford Language, the term validation means "recognition or affirmation that a person or their feelings or opinions are valid or worthwhile." Support means "bear all or part of the weight of; hold up."

I have quite literally spent most of my life looking for someone to validate my every move. I thought I was seeking support from family and loved ones. I thought I was looking for them to encourage. Truthfully, however, I was looking for others to assure me that my actions or efforts were worthwhile.

If I am being honest, I did not notice this until I was in my thirties. I wholeheartedly thought I was simply seeking support when choosing to make a life change or decision. But when I look back at my life, I can barely tell when I started living for myself and my dreams.

Yes, you can say it was when I decided to drop out of grad school, started working for an international resort company, and traveled the world that I started living for myself, but if you remember, my parents both worked for the same company. They met while working for the company, fell in love, got married, and had me. I think somewhere in my mind, this was a path I knew I could possibly take with full support. I think it gave me validation that my parents would be proud of me for taking that path.

As it turned out, they supported me when I went to grad school, while I worked hard toward my goal of completing my master's, but they did not give me the validation I needed in regard to my career choice.

We live in a society where we are hyper-focused and hyper-aware of what other people think about us. We find ourselves feeling defeated when someone does not "support" our life decision or choices, when in reality, we might actually be seeking their "validation."

Maybe this has not impacted your career choice, but what about an individual you've dated? You introduce them to your friends and family, bring them into your world, and show everyone how much they mean to you, and then you ask your loved ones, "So what do you think?"

We want their support, we want them to like our significant other—but I believe more often than not, we are seeking validation that this person is possibly suitable as a potential life partner. Gaining support is one thing, but it doesn't always feel like enough—we need to feel validated that we made the right choice.

It could be something as small as buying a new couch too. We love it, we put it in the living room, and we finally have friends and family over to see it. I think most of us would agree that we

We find ourselves feeling defeated when someone does not "support" our life decision or choices, when in reality, we might actually be seeking their "validation."

are seeking their validation that we made the right choice. We need them all to think it looks great and validate our decision. Obviously, a couch is a minor detail compared to an intended life decision! But it seems that for many of us, that need for validation is always an underlying occurrence.

Unfortunately, the area of life where we most often seek validation is our self-worth. We often rely on the validation of others to believe in ourselves. This can be in our home life, our relationships, or our career. We find ourselves solely relying on the validation of others before we believe we are making the right decisions for ourselves.

For me, this simply stemmed from lack of confidence. Every move I made throughout life, I constantly wondered what other people were thinking. I wanted approval. No wonder I have had so much anxiety throughout most of my life. I quite literally have not been living for myself!

Maybe this is you. Maybe you need your boss to validate your self-worth and you've been waiting for that positive reinforcement to let you know that a promotion is on the horizon. But I'm going to tell you this: your hard work is enough, and you do not need recognition from on high to keep going. What you do need is to keep showing up and to know that your hard work is being recognized regardless of the affirmation you feel you require.

In romantic relationships, this works just the same: it's possible you feel your partner is not complimenting you or showing you the affection you need in order for you to hold your head high with confidence. Instead, put on that makeup or that favorite shirt and remember to own your confidence. It's not about the compliment we are hoping to receive; it's about thinking highly of ourselves and knowing we hold the ability to give ourselves the validation we crave. After all, your partner most likely started dating you or fell in love with you for the personality or characteristics you possess, so let them shine rather than tucking them away while you wait for them to be confirmed.

We will never have everyone's support. We will never have every single individual validate our every move, nor should we want that. People will disagree with us. People will not see eye to eye with how we choose to live our lives. But isn't that what makes us an individual? Isn't that what keeps conversation going and allows for all our differences to be beautiful and unique?

> *"If outside validation is your only source of nourishment, you will be hungry for the rest of your life."*
> **—Author unknown**

Don't get me wrong, I think we all have that ex we're glad our friends told us the truth about, but hey, if you love your huge, oversized couch that your dad says is not practical, grab your blanket, grab the pups, and cuddle up to enjoy that beauty!

In all seriousness, I think it is important and extremely valuable to check in with ourselves and ask if we are seeking support or validation in prominent areas of our lives. If we continue to seek validation for every decision we make, we'll never live happy or fulfilling lives, let alone lives that are our own.

If we continue to seek validation for every decision we make, we'll never live happy or fulfilling lives, let alone lives that are our own.

CHAPTER NINE

What Do They Want? versus What Do I Want?

Do you ever feel as though the days and weeks are one big blur? I swear I wake up sometimes and whole months have come and gone! While some days drag on as if there is no end, chunks of time pass by without anything actually getting done. Sure, the weekly to-do lists somehow find check marks next to each task, but it is more out of habit, not out of intention.

Sometimes I can give myself a solid "Heck yes!" after a specifically challenging season of life and feel damn proud that I made it through! But there have been several times like this where I have to stop and ask myself, who am I living for? Who am I waking up for each and every day? Am I even showing up for myself?

Of course, we all do things that we don't necessarily want to do, and obviously life requires doing things for others whether or not they're someone we would choose to help on our own. I may work for myself now, but I have had plenty of bosses over the years that were the fuel behind eye rolls and to-do lists that I had zero interest in. But that's just part of life.

However, it's so easy to wake up and let the to-do list or stringent routine dictate our day, even though there is very rarely any part of the list that's for ourselves. The needs that allow us to grow and feel accomplished at the end of the day are pushed to the side.

Everyone has a regimented to-do list, but maybe you have been so consumed by the needs and requirements of others that you haven't had time to establish the actions needed to care for yourself.

When you get on a plane, they take you through the safety procedures in the case of an emergency and remind you to put on your own oxygen mask before assisting others with their mask. But in real life, how many of us would take the time to adjust our own oxygen mask properly before helping our kiddos or loved ones? We are constantly assisting others, which truly does speak volumes about our character, but at what cost? Who do we become if we stop paying attention to our own needs? Anyone else still pushing aside the growth and development goals we intended to start three New Year's resolutions ago? I'm going to assume many of you reading this are sighing or laughing to yourself, saying, "Yep, sounds about right."

I do not know what it will take for many of us to start realizing that time is simply passing by with little to none of our intention being placed on ourselves. Either our goals and dreams begin to slip away, or we fall victim to changing them to align a bit more with the daily tasks that seem to consume us.

For me, it took finally asking myself one simple question: "What do they want?" versus "What do I want?"

I am very guilty of being a people pleaser. Partly because I really do enjoy making others happy! I enjoy being a part of other people's lives and some-

Either our goals and dreams begin to slip away, or we fall victim to changing them to align a bit more with the daily tasks that seem to consume us.

how leaving them feeling a little more fulfilled than before, but that's partly because I do not like to disappoint anyone.

In the past, before nearly every new situation or obstacle, I unknowingly asked myself the question, "Well, what do they want? What would make them happy or proud?" This was what led to many of my big decisions, from athletics to career choices. I wasn't thinking about what I needed, so I started to lose my sense of self and independence.

I wanted to impress my coaches, so I made choices that I thought would fit the plan they saw unfolding for me. I wound up seeing a sports psychologist because I was crippled in the start gate before every downhill snow ski race. I was terrified about my impending performance and what my parents and coaches would think.

It has been over thirteen years since I last clicked my boots into my bindings for a race, and to this day I wonder where the sport would have taken me had I not been so worried about others' perceptions of me. Sadly, I think I would have exceeded any expectation someone else had of me as well as my own expectations, but instead paralysis took over.

This fear and hesitation occurred with my education too. I desperately wanted to impress my parents and grandparents with my academic abilities, so as mentioned, I pursued grad school after college. I later found out that my parents actually would have preferred me to take a step back from my need to be perfect and thought I'd be happier had I simply left the country right away to travel. But again, I wasn't asking anyone what they thought I should do—I was assuming what they wanted for me.

What about relationships? Are you in a relationship that fits your current lifestyle, assuming your partner is the one? Everything just seems to "work," but maybe there is something missing. In past relationships, I often assumed that if my life looked like it could pan out the way I expected, I must be with the right person, despite having a feeling that something was off.

Many of us are consumed by such assumptions to the extent that they dictate numerous important decisions in our life. Whether it is in your relationship, your health and fitness journey, your line of work, or your hesitation to take steps toward your dreams, it is important to ask ourselves whether we are acting out of what they want or what we want.

Initially, my assumptions of how others wanted me to live my life got the best of me at a pivotal point in life, so I ended up leaving the country and falling in love with someone.

Now, I am not telling you to up and leave the life you currently are living! We all know my story was much messier than that. I somehow found myself in my midtwenties still making every move based on what others wanted for me or what I assumed they wanted for me.

Finally, when I turned twenty-nine, I began to ask myself, "What do I want?"

Life did not magically turn around, but I will say things slowly shifted. This was the first time I started to learn about myself. I started to take a deeper look into who I was as a person and all the qualities I had to offer myself and everyone around me!

I did not do this on my own—I sought the help of a therapist, as you know. I was very concerned about the judgment from others, but that judgment never came.

Slowly but surely, I took my own goals and dreams into consideration. I would ask myself, "What do I want?" I started to break down the hopes and desires I had for myself and create intentional steps to make sure they came to fruition. Of course, some goals were going to take longer than others, but the steps to see them through were finally coming to fruition.

This was also a time when I stopped comparing myself to others in a way that was genuinely impacting who I was as an individual! Being in the space of social media, it can be easy to unknowingly start to take on qualities and characteristics of others. It is important that I continue to grow and evolve as an individual, but I noticed that I was losing sight of some of my wonderful qualities because I thought others would make me more desirable to certain companies I wanted to work with or to my community.

I am sure some of you can relate! You might also feel the impact of social media, whether it is on your own personality, the clothes you wear, the workouts you do, or even the career you are working toward. I believe it is normal to be impacted by social media in today's society, but it is also important to check in with ourselves to really analyze just how much it is impacting us and in what way. For me, I was losing a sense of self and starting to show up according to the mold I thought I was supposed to shape myself with.

I think the big mental shift came after having our son Cayden, when I finally started to fully lean into who I am as a person and which direction I want to evolve in, whether in life or in business.

The mindset shift was all I needed. I am fully aware that I will forever be a people pleaser on some level, and I am entirely okay with that! I think it helps me accomplish things beyond my own ability because I set higher standards for myself. However, my daily actions and everyday to-do lists are now more focused on my own hopes and dreams rather than fulfilling those of others.

It is easy to get lost in helping others reach their goals and encouraging them to do their best, but we forget to encourage ourselves. We forget to take inventory on where we are at in our life. As Tony Gaskins said, "If you don't build your dream, someone else will hire you to build theirs."

So take inventory! When was the last time you even sat down to write down your goals? Not just think about them, but physically write them down! Make them come to life on the page before you! Create a to-do list based on each one of the goals and dreams you have for yourself. Make the steps actionable and intentional, but also realistic. Tell someone about them! Ask them to hold you accountable, to check in with you to make sure you are continuing to take daily steps.

Living for yourself will take time. It will not happen overnight. I am thirty-one years old and still working on making this shift. We need to recognize that building takes time! It is a long process that can be messy and uncertain, but in the end, you get a beautiful masterpiece.

If you are lying in bed or taking some "you" time while reading this book, take inventory. Right now! Are you building your dreams?

I challenge you to ask yourself the questions that can help you establish your sense of self and independence. Lead yourself away from "What do they want?" toward "What do I want?"

So, tell me this: which question did you start to answer first?

We need to recognize that building takes time! It is a long process that can be messy and uncertain, but in the end, you get a beautiful masterpiece.

CHAPTER TEN

Made for This

I have clearly spent the majority of my life running someone else's race. Something always felt off, but I kept taking steps forward because I thought it was the track I was supposed to be on.

This has been a struggle of mine at many points in my life without my even knowing!

Figuring out our path and our race is not easy by any means. For me, this inability to see my own race or a path perfectly designed for me kept me from taking the necessary strides forward in the life I was created for. I continued to feel this unknown stress and anxiety weighing me down.

This feeling of almost running in place spilled over into my marriage, my business, my parenting, my ability to be a friend. When we get wrapped up in running other people's races or attempting

When we get
wrapped up in
running other
people's races
or attempting
to emulate
them, we get
lost, because
that path wasn't
made for us.

to emulate them, we get lost, because that path wasn't made for us.

Let me ask you, have you ever worked hard at something but had everything feel so wrong that the pieces just wouldn't seem to ever fall into place? Maybe a little imposter syndrome? Gosh, part of me feels it as I write these words—technically, I am not a "writer"—but this book is about the message and relatability so many of us have despite being on different journeys.

I want to tell you a story about the time my husband, Casey, and I started a business together. We were only dating at the time; we had just moved back from working for Club Med for multiple years and were trying to find our direction in life. Before giving you more details on this part of our story, I want to share that most of our drive behind finding our direction in life was fueled by wanting to be "successful." I use quotes around "successful" because there was an unspoken need between us for "success" to translate into monetary success. We also assumed that we needed to find this direction quickly—we had taken lots of time to travel with Club Med, so "adulting" had been pushed aside.

I grew up with two parents who worked extremely hard in all aspects of life but especially in their business endeavors. We did not have much growing up, but I watched them work daily to create the lifestyle they now have and the opportunities they provided for me and my sister. Watching my parents work day in and day out for their financial success ingrained something in me that I admire. It taught me about hard work and determination, and that success is not always linear. You will fail along the way, but that does not mean you are "failing" or a "failure." You learn from it, pivot, and continue taking the next steps forward.

As I watched my parents grow in monetary success, I saw their lifestyle slowly change from being very cautious with money to being able to donate to their favorite organizations, give back to the community, and financially assist me through college. It was at that point that I think I began to associate success with money.

And might I add, that aside from my parents, we

now live in a world where we can open our phones and see the assumed success of others. New homes, new cars, shopping sprees. It can feel like we are constantly needing to strive for more and this concept of "more" continued to put monetary association with success.

This did not impact me initially. I stayed my course, got my degree in early childhood and family studies and continued on to get my master's in school counseling before, as you know, I dropped out and took a different direction. In that season of my life, I was not looking for monetary success but rather the title that would uphold conversations and on some level make me feel fulfilled.

But here I was, late twenties, back from my travels, dating a man I intended to marry but had never actually discussed marriage with, and a flattering business opportunity was presented to us.

I always learned that it "takes money to make money," so while the initial investment was daunting, when we sat down with the business owner and discussed our sales strategies, I think Casey and I only saw very attractive numbers and what I would describe at the time as "success."

So, after about a year and a half of business development and the build-out of a custom food trailer, we hit the ground running our first summer in business and attended events all over Washington state. With help from our incredible friends, we did not have to pay employees that first summer, but we worked harder than I had ever worked in my life. We all pulled twenty-four-hour shifts at some of the events. We ate our soft-serve product for breakfast, lunch, and dinner. We even had our parents working in our commissary kitchen until late hours of the night helping us prepare everything for our very first event.

Needless to say, we had amazing support, a lot of drive, and a willingness to work! But we then came to find out the machine that made the soft serve was unable to work properly due to inadequate power at these remote locations.

In sum, the machine that was the primary source behind our business model was failing us. At every event, at every hour of the day, our livelihood would break down on us.

So here we were, with a fully outfitted custom food trailer, a truck to pull the trailer, and a container full of ten pallets of product we were intending to distribute to other businesses, and the "success" we were looking for was nowhere in sight. We were an unmarried couple who were hundreds of thousands of dollars in debt. Let that one sink in. I can look back and laugh now (almost), but what were we thinking?

We spent the next year doing smaller events closer to home and reworking every angle of our business model, only to end up closing our business after three short but very long years of operation. We took a lot of time to self-reflect and held many business meetings with my parents to learn from our mistakes and create a plan to get out of debt, but the feeling of failure loomed over us.

You see, we saw a path, a race that seemed worth running. All the elements were there! Everything was laid out for us in such a way that screamed, "Go for it! Why not us?!" But deep down, if Casey and I both had to admit, we were taking the easy route to what we saw as "success"—monetary success.

Now, let me also acknowledge that I don't know if I would have realized this wasn't my race to run until after the fact—hindsight is 20/20. But I do know that passion did not fuel this race. Purpose did not fuel this race. And that tiny feeling in my gut that I kept suppressing was what I should have been listening to all along.

It has been about three years since that business endeavor closed, and I finally feel like I am on my path and running my race. The work that I have put into this path has in many ways been harder than the long nights and debt of the food trailer life, but it has been fueled by a completely different drive.

It is a path that, at most times, truly has not been supported by my family due to lack of understanding. Sometimes our paths and our decisions throughout life do not make sense to other people or to those who love us, and that is okay! Those hurdles and struggles are worth pushing through if the feeling in your gut is telling you to keep running, keep pushing!

This feeling for you might not be a business endeavor. It might not be within sports or athletics. But maybe it is within your relationship. Maybe it is within your own health and fitness journey. Whose race are you running?

However many races you have been running, don't stop! We all get confused or uncertain about which path has our name on it. Simply reevaluate and find your race.

As Christine Caine said, "So evaluate how you're running your race. Make any adjustments necessary. Run your race well, because you were made for this!" And as one of my favorite mentors, Sal Frisella, always says, "Left foot, right foot." It will be hard, you can almost guarantee it will be messy, but keep taking the steps!

Simply
reevaluate
and find
your race.

CHAPTER ELEVEN

Maybe "Waiting Is the Hardest Part"

Do you ever feel like you're searching for that "perfect" job? Or trying to figure out where exactly you are "supposed" to be in this world? It's as if every day we wake up in search of something, never feeling satisfied unless we find it.

For as long as I can remember, I have constantly been trying to see what's around the corner and pursue the next opportunity that is "supposed" to be on my path. I never feel content with just being in the "now."

Don't get me wrong—I'm a goal setter, but part of this requires a little bit of thought on how to get to those goals and what they might look like. It can be exciting to manifest our hopes and dreams for ourselves, but rather than taking things one step at a time, I try to sprint the whole damn mile and end up overwhelmed and extremely lost.

Over the years, feeling the need to be someone or something and putting that pressure on myself has taken me in every direction other than the path I want to be on. Now, in my thirties, I'm still not entirely sure what I truly want, but I no longer want the anxiety of the winding road to take away from the life I am currently living.

When we think about our lives, there are many moments that are "supposed" to take place. It is easy to lose ourselves in these moments, or better yet, to wait around for these moments to happen. These are events that are ingrained in us, milestones that must be remembered. They are the memories we hear our parents and grandparents recalling from their past, which leads to us asking ourselves all sorts of questions:

"Will I ever graduate from college with my degree?"

"Will I ever meet the person that I am supposed to spend my life with?"

"When will this person I've been dating for the last half a decade get down on one knee?"

"Will I ever have enough money to buy that house?"

"When will all my hard work pay off and get me that promotion?"

"Will I ever see the positive blue plus sign on a pregnancy test?"

I get it. There is a lot to be waiting for! Some of it comes with excitement, while other moments come with a lot of heartache.

Some of these moments of anxiety or uncertainty we choose not to share with people in our life; instead, they become bottled up and feed into that feeling of "waiting" for whatever is supposed to happen next.

I believe many of us are waiting for these memorable moments because they give us something to share with our loved ones. They help us answer the question "So what do you do?"

There have been many times in my life where this sense of waiting has consumed me.

In my relationship, I swear my husband would

never get down on one knee. It took me asking him after two years of dating how I should introduce him to others, because we had never used the terms "boyfriend" or "girlfriend" before. True story! We were heading on a road trip down the coast of California and would be couch surfing a bit, staying with family and friends along the way. I looked at him in the car and simply asked how I should introduce him to some of the people he had never met before.

Clearly, I wanted him to say, "Well, as your boyfriend, of course!" But remember, this wasn't a Nicholas Sparks book. He answered with a vague statement that I could introduce him however I wanted to. I think I responded, irked, that I would be introducing him as my boyfriend.

I mean, come on! We had been dating for nearly two years, and we were about to move to Japan together for another position with Club Med. We would be sharing a room! Didn't that define us as boyfriend and girlfriend?

Another struggle for me was the fact that we only talked about marriage one time before getting engaged! Once! We had just moved back from Club Med. After attending a number of weddings over the summer, I finally asked him as we sat on the couch, "Are we ever going to get married?"

He looked at me and casually said, "Yeah, why? Do you not want to?"

I wish you could have seen the total surprise on my face. I responded, "Of course I want to, but we've never talked about it."

He simply said, "There's nothing to talk about. We're going to get married."

I wish I could insert an eye roll here. And don't get too excited, ladies—he didn't propose after that for over a year! We dated for five years before the proposal finally came.

There were so many moments where I felt like I was just waiting for it to happen. I am sure many of you are either nodding your head or sighing in recognition!

One thing Casey did share with me was that as a man, he struggled with feeling like things needed to be perfect or put together before he was able to get down on one knee. From asking the father for his daughter's hand in marriage to picking out the ring to organizing/planning a proposal, he felt like he needed to be at a certain place in life before he could pop the question.

I think my struggle with our lack of communication on this topic came because my mind jumped to assuming he did not want to marry me or was still unsure—in reality, we just had different timelines!

Possibly, your story is on the complete flip side. Maybe marriage is not something you're "waiting" for! We all have different experiences with our partners, and I believe the main point is that we must recognize that the story is not one-size-fits-all. Heck, I am still working on starting a relationship with myself, which is probably the most important relationship of them all!

But, as with so many other things in life, when it came to me and Casey, I was not taking all the little details into consideration, just waiting! Waiting for that next step in life to take place so we could keep on living.

Over the course of the five years before Casey proposed, we had so many unbelievable moments!

I mean, unreal! First of all, I couldn't believe how in love with him I was. Second of all, we were quite literally traveling the world together for a portion of that time! He's an unbelievable human, someone who was challenging me in ways that took me out of my comfort zone, someone I continued to learn from and grow with—yet I was waiting for titles, for the next "step" in the relationship, and missing out on the little details that we would remember forever.

When we're waiting for something, we stop living, and we fail to recognize the little moments that are happening right before us.

But why do we stop living in the first place? Why do we constantly look to see what is down the road or up around the corner? Why do we go through the motions until the next step takes place?

* * *

The world Casey and I had built after our marriage came to a screeching halt when I experienced a miscarriage at 11.5 weeks with our first little bundle. Looking back on it, every little part of that pregnancy felt like a waiting game.

"How many days until I can take the first pregnancy test?" "How long do I wait until the plus sign appears blue?" "When do we tell our family?" "When is the first ultrasound?" "How long until we can announce on social media?"

And then it was all taken away. In that moment, I realized I had just spent nearly three months focusing on the next part of the pregnancy and being able to announce it so it would be "real." It was real the entire time! I simply hadn't taken the time to be in the moment.

I'm sure you can believe the waiting game started all over again after the miscarriage. But something switched for me. The miscarriage led to a lot of self-reflection and time to think. I had truly been living my life waiting for what was coming and not experiencing my day-to-day life. What was next? Would it bring excitement? Would it bring heartbreak? How could I plan for it?

We are not supposed to be able to plan for everything! Can we be prepared? Maybe, but planning for something we hope or want to happen is nearly impossible!

So, are you waiting for the proposal? Are you waiting for the promotion? Are you waiting for the scale to display a lower number? Are you waiting for the positive blue sign to finally show up?

We all are waiting for something, and waiting is the hardest part! The unknown is the most exciting yet daunting thing ever. But when do we start appreciating where we are? When do we allow ourselves to be in the moment and do our best each and every day?

If we are constantly waiting for what's next, are we ever actually living? Sometimes the feeling of waiting can be numbing because our ability to be present is nearly impossible, but if we can start with appreciating where we are, some of that unknown can become exciting! I love this quote by Charles Stanley: "Our willingness to wait reveals the value we place on what we are waiting for . . ."

Stop waiting for your boss to give you the promotion—work as though you already have it!

Stop waiting for your boyfriend or girlfriend to

get down on one knee—be the future wife or husband that your significant other would be lucky to put a ring on!

Stop waiting for the scale to go down—get into an intentional workout, nourish your mind and body, and show up for yourself today!

Life is uncertain! The road map is not perfect, nor is it supposed to be. If you find yourself working toward something based off what is going on in other people's lives or set impossible expectations for yourself, you will never feel accomplished.

Turning thirty does not mean you need to be married, own a home, have two kids, and be deep into a career. I am thirty-one, renting a home, and have two dogs, a newborn baby, and zero idea what my job title is, let alone know how to explain what I do to anyone in my parents' generation.

Appreciate where you are, not where you think you are supposed to be. I can guarantee you that the social media influencer you admire has his/her own ticket on the Hot Mess Express as well!

Waiting is hard, the unknown is hard, but life is

Appreciate where you are, not where you think you are supposed to be.

not meant to be easy. The easy route should not be our goal. Choose crazy, embrace it!

CHAPTER TWELVE

The Journey Is Not the Glamorous Part

Starting from the beginning is not always how things are supposed to unfold.

We learn to read a book from beginning to end or write on a piece of paper from top to bottom, but life is not always as clear and concise as that.

For instance, when you fill out your daily planner, sometimes it doesn't work to write in your morning activities until you have worked backward from filling out afternoon priorities first. When you fill out the family calendar hanging on your wall, you might block off a week of vacation six months from now as well as fill in every Tuesday and Thursday for soccer practice.

As you can see, life itself often does not unfold

from top to bottom, or in the neat and orderly fashion we would hope or expect it to unfold in.

This is exactly how our goals and intentions for ourselves work as well! We get so down when a specific timeline we have mapped out for ourselves does not come to fruition as we had planned. In reality, things are falling into place exactly as we had hoped, just with a few unexpected occurrences. We let these roadblocks or detours in the life map we have laid out for ourselves stop us, rather than opening our eyes and seeing how other opportunities might be showing up along the way.

Similar to filling out our planner, when we write down our goals or expectations, we sometimes have them in an order that makes sense for us and the life we envision for ourselves. For instance: go to college, meet your person, fall in love, graduate, start a job, get married, and maybe start a family.

Of course, this is the fairy-tale timeline of Disney days and very different from the reality many of us are living in, which is entirely okay! It took a lot of rewriting and editing of my own story for me to accept the changes my life map took on over the years.

I swear, sometimes I feel like everyone around me has it all figured out and seems to be so put together! I have so many individuals I look up to, but I don't think my narrative or steps to success will ever align with theirs! It has taken me numerous self-help books and so many "restarts" on my journey to finally see that our steps are not supposed to line up to theirs. We are not supposed to be able to copy and paste someone else's life and apply it to our own actions—we have to create our path.

Yes, we can take some tips from these individuals, learn from them, and apply their knowledge to what we are trying to achieve in our own life. After all, they are successful for a reason, so taking some of their advice and expertise can be extremely helpful!

But more often than not, the information or advice we are consuming is all hindsight. Our self-help book is written from the point of view of an individual who has reached point B. They share how they made it from point A to point B and allow us to see it as a doable task. We read this self-help book from beginning to end because that's how the book unfolds, but that does not mean that's how the author's story really unfolded.

Don't get me wrong, of course they share the hard moments! They illuminate the parts where they had to put their goal or dream before anything else while others in their life gave up on them or did not believe in them. But very rarely do we look to someone for advice or help while they are actually in the thick of it.

We don't grab the self-help book about someone on the road from point A to point B, because it's messy, it's uncertain, it's unclear! And success is not glorified in those books. In fact, those books don't even seem to exist. People don't usually want to be along for the journey; the journey is not the glamorous part. They want to ask all the questions and know the secrets once they've achieved what they deem as success.

Today's society so badly wants to achieve success with as little work as possible. We live in a world where there is almost instant gratification, and we assume we can put forth minimal effort to reach our goals and dreams. I swear some people put all their thought and effort into finding a way to achieve their dreams with as little work as possible, rather than just putting in the work. In the same amount of time, they could have been halfway there.

I don't think it's their fault—we no longer see or hear about the journey, but I think it is because we choose not to look for it or watch it. Many people do achieve success with minimal efforts. Social media allows for some to quite literally have overnight success. But this should not take away from our ability to work hard or push through the struggles we are experiencing to reach our hopes and dreams.

Recently, I have had to ask myself: am I capable of hard work? I know I am, but as seasons of my life have evolved, hard work looks and feels different. If I am being completely honest, I think I am somewhat afraid of it.

When we put all our efforts into one specific goal, the opportunity for failure presents itself. We

We can want something so badly, we can wish for it daily, but if we do not put in the hard work, we are simply standing still.

can want something so badly, we can wish for it daily, but if we do not put in the hard work, we are simply standing still.

However, not taking that step forward allows us to remain in a place where we feel "safe." It is known, and we are comfortable. Taking a step, starting a journey, requires us to get out of our comfort zone.

As I stated earlier, the journey from point A to point B can be messy and unclear. This is where the hard work lies; this is where the journey truly shines. It will not unfold from left to right and most likely will require you to jump all over the page to figure it out.

If you are anything like me, this is also where the paralysis by analysis settles in. I recognize the journey ahead of me, I know it will take hard work, but I often freeze when I see the number of steps and/ or amount of time it will take to reach the specific goal I am striving for.

But guess what? We do not need to start from the beginning. We do not need to start at step one in order to get to step ten. If that first task is what you are getting caught up on, move on to the next one! Come back to it later! It will still be there, but now you'll have a different mindset or view on what it will take to get it done.

Tell yourself you will achieve all your goals. Once you arrive at the destination you have been striving for, that is when people will ask how you managed to get there. Some people will be along for the journey, while others will join you once the goal is achieved. The journey is not the alluring part. It's the glitz and glam. It's the "fit" body. It's the stunning beach vacation. But don't miss out on the journey. If you believe you can, then you will!

We are worthy of taking the steps toward our wildest dreams. We are worthy of hard work and determination that most definitely will scare us at times.

It's the moments people don't see behind the scenes. It's the moments that sometimes make us feel like we are taking two steps forward, then three steps back and to the side. It's the moments that make us question what the heck we are doing striving for this goal or dream. But keep taking the small steps. Keep showing up for yourself and your goals.

> *"You wish and you dream with all your heart. But remember, that old star can only take you part of the way. You got to help it with some hard work of your own. And then you can do anything you set your mind to."*
> —**Tiana's father, *The Princess and the Frog***

Don't let the hard work discourage you. Don't let the unknowns of the journey keep you from taking the first step.

Take the step.

CHAPTER THIRTEEN

Show Up for Yourself

When I met my husband, my life was forever changed. He has truly been a blessing, all my wishes wrapped up into one human. Don't get me wrong, it hasn't been easy! We are very opposite in so many ways and have completely different love languages, but it's been worth it.

Throughout life, we typically encounter some individuals that will build us up, some that will tear us down, and others that will make us want to better ourselves simply by their presence. My husband has been one of those individuals who has unknowingly made me want to be a better version of myself. He has always made me want to show up as my best self!

When we first met, I simply showed up as myself. I was young and had a drive and zest for life that was exciting, taking me on journeys that I never imagined! However, I was still trying to figure out who I was as an individual, and I was extremely uncertain about the direction my life was heading in. I was enjoying myself and truly didn't have a focus on intentional self-growth, but when I was around Casey, I wanted him to see me at my best—not out of fear of letting him see me at my worst, but because he brought out the best in me. He made me want to be better!

After we had finally started dating and eventually moved home, we got into a routine. I wouldn't say the butterflies went away, but complacency set in and we got comfortable. I was working on career growth as well as adjusting to life back home, but somewhere I stopped working on myself as an individual. I lost a bit of the self-awareness and intention that used to create a drive to show up as a better version of myself for tomorrow.

Let me ask you, who do you show up as on a first date or for a job interview? Think about it for a moment: how you walk into the room, how you present yourself, how you carry on the conversation. I know it's definitely a pretty great version of myself that shows up to the occasion.

Now ask yourself, what version of you is showing up in your current life? Whether it is in a relationship, your workout program, or your job, do you have that energy and presence that you started with initially?

Of course, things change and comfort sets in a bit, but when does that shift to a little laziness or lack of care? I am writing this while sitting on our couch in an oversized T-shirt, no pants, and with hair that has not been washed in a number of days. It's almost 11:00 a.m. Does this paint you a nice picture? While mornings like this are totally fine, I have realized they've become my norm.

I might show up as what I think is the best self I'm capable of achieving that day, but truthfully, I don't leave myself much time to reflect on whether I am taking that extra step each day to better myself. Sometimes we think these extra steps will be time consuming and overwhelming, so we bump them down the to-do list. In reality, they take minimal effort, and usually in less time than we spend contemplating them!

When I first started saying "show up for yourself" or "show up as your best self," it really did feel consuming! It felt like a lot of pressure to try to be my absolute best self every day. Let's be honest, sometimes it's nice to throw on the oversized sweats, put the hair in a messy bun, take the bra off, and just sit on the couch! That type of day screams my name sometimes!

But what if we rephrased things? What if we showed up as our best self for that day? Every day is going to look and feel different. What might be our "best self" one day could be entirely different the next! Give yourself some grace and recognize that showing up for yourself, presenting the best version of yourself, is going to look and feel different from day to day. However, I think it is imperative we check in with ourselves and see who we are showing up as, not who we are showing up for.

Showing up as our best self is for ourselves! Not for anyone else! As I have clearly outlined in this book, all too often we are living for others. We are

Give yourself
some grace
and recognize
that showing
up for yourself,
presenting the best
version of yourself,
is going to look
and feel different
from day to day.

working toward their goals, their dreams for us, their expectations, which ends up overshadowing who we are supposed to be.

I have heard from a number of mentors and read in a number of my self-help books that I should surround myself with the hardest workers in the room, or people who are smarter, stronger, and more successful than me, in order to grow or be a better version of myself. While I do not disagree with this—I know that I would not be where I am today without my mentors or those I look up to and learn from—it can be challenging sometimes. I believe we all go through seasons where we feel alone. We feel as though we do not have anyone to turn to, so when we turn to ourselves, we don't know where to start. We don't know how to push ourselves to be better.

I always try to tell myself to take things one day at a time, one step at a time. It can be overwhelming when we look at the entire week ahead of us or all the steps needed to reach our goal, but if we break it down, it becomes more doable. Similarly, in a workout, if we look at all the exercises that are programmed for that day, we get overwhelmed, and often we just go through the motions rather than being intentional. However, if we break it down to each individual rep of each set of one exercise, we can be intentional about that one rep in front of us and perform it to our best ability.

To start showing up for yourself, you need to take things one day at a time. Create actionable, daily steps toward your goals and dreams that make them more attainable. One day at a time, yes! But one day at a time with intention.

This will take hard work. It will be uncomfortable. But showing up for yourself, being the best version of yourself for that day, will allow you to show up as your best self for others! How can you continue to show up for everything and everyone else if you don't show up for yourself? A life that once was focused on what other people expected of you has now become about what you expect of yourself. Don't settle.

But one day
at a time with
intention.

CHAPTER FOURTEEN

Don't Stop, Just Rewrite

The expectations we hold on to in life often do not unfold into our reality, but that does not mean we stop. We simply take that next step and continue writing our story. A lot of us start writing our story before it's even happened. We expect certain things to happen, right? But as we know, expectations and reality are very different.

Who is currently planning their wedding, but not actually engaged? Maybe you are designing your new office but have not yet received the promotion. Or maybe you drive around the neighborhood that you do not live in yet, but the corner lot and fence you will have around your house are all picked out.

Let's not get confused—I fully believe in the power of manifesting! I write down moments and goals in my life as if they have already happened and manifest the heck out of them! I have my dream kitchen all planned out, my future yearly family vacations written out in detail, and my fantasy car parked in our future garage. I genuinely write goals down as if they have already happened in my current life. There is so much incredible value in manifesting, and it has allowed me to push harder in moments where my "why" and my life path are both a little unclear. However, the expectation of how these manifestations come to fruition is not typically how reality unfolds, and there are many struggles along the way.

For many of us, struggles and vulnerabilities have held us back in life or kept us at a standstill. Up until this point in the book, I have illuminated seasons and moments in our lives that have defined us, consumed us, and at times made us think less of ourselves. The story we wrote for our life has not unfolded as we intended, which has left many of us uncertain about where we are and where we are going—at times, uncertain of who we even are as individuals.

But what if we strip back the narrative? What if we allow ourselves to simply rewrite?

The beautiful chapters you have written for yourself do not need to be deleted; they need some minor (or at times major) edits, but the book does not end. Our stories do not become any less valuable or less important.

The rewrite can be hard, though. It can be scary and leave us doubting our own abilities. At times, it can also lead us to question our happiness or what it is supposed to look like in our life. We have become so consumed by the story we have written for ourselves that we do not know how to see beyond the current moment. But truthfully, all we need to do is take the step.

I want to place emphasis on "take the step." When we hear people say, "Just take that next step," or, "You've got this, all you need to do is start," we can take it too literally and set ourselves up for failure. Sometimes "taking the step" does not happen in an organized manner. As Robert Brault says, sometimes the forward direction we are intending to go somehow ends up resembling the cha-cha or

The beautiful chapters you have written for yourself do not need to be deleted; they need some minor (or at times major) edits, but the book does not end.

Cupid Shuffle, veering to the side, backward, and sometimes adding a spin in there.

Of course, this is beyond frustrating! For me, as you know, these seasons are where I typically fall into my paralysis by analysis. I end up complacent, pushing aside the hard work that would lead me to self-growth as well as that next chapter I am trying to write for myself. But in these moments—because there will be multiple times throughout life that this happens—know you are not alone! Know that your story has just begun. Your next chapter might be messy, but it is all part of the story in getting you to where you are working on going.

This might require you to do things afraid! Don't wait until the absence of fear becomes present; that may never happen. Let that fear be your fuel and drive to push forward.

> *"Courage doesn't mean you don't get afraid. Courage means you don't let fear stop you."*
> —**Bethany Hamilton**

Much of this is easier said than done. Between Nicholas Sparks and Disney, many of us are waiting for a fairy tale or perfectly curated story to unfold. But if we take back control of who is writing our story, maybe, just maybe, we can be the author of our own life.

About the Author

Carly-Ann Dell is a health and wellness enthusiast who dropped out of grad school to travel the world—and discovered her real passion for helping others. Today she is the host of the Crazy Over Easy podcast, where she talks about recognizing that life is not a one size fits all. Carly-Ann lives with her husband, kids, and spirited dogs in Lake Stevens, Washington. For more real talk, travel stories, and fitness resources meant to fit real lives, visit CarlyAnnDell.com. Follow her on Instagram and Pinterest at @carlyanndell.